# What's Inside

# Racing Cars

**W**
**FRANKLIN WATTS**
LONDON • SYDNEY

Franklin Watts
First published in Great Britain in 2016 by The Watts Publishing Group

Designed and illustrated by David West

Dewey number 629.2'28-dc23
HB ISBN 978 1 4451 4620 1

Printed in Malaysia

Franklin Watts
An imprint of
Hachette Children's Group
Part of The Watts Publishing Group
Carmelite House
50 Victoria Embankment
London EC4Y 0DZ

An Hachette UK Company
www.hachette.co.uk

www.franklinwatts.co.uk

WHAT'S INSIDE RACING CARS
was produced for Franklin Watts by
David West Children's Books, 6 Princeton Court, 55 Felsham Road, London SW15 1AZ

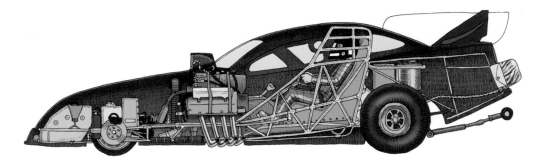

# Contents

The First Racers **4**

1903 Mercedes **6**

Single-seaters **8**

Alfa Romeo P3 **10**

Modern Open-wheelers **12**

Formula Car **14**

Stock Car Racers **16**

NASCAR Stock Car **18**

Drag Racers **20**

Funny Car **22**

Glossary and Index **24**

# The First Racers

Car racing began in the 1880s, soon after the invention of the petrol **internal combustion engine**. These racing machines had large wheels with rubber tyres and the back wheels were chain-driven. The cars, which averaged speeds of 24 to 32 kph, were unreliable and often broke down.

*This 1903 Mercedes, driven by the Belgian racer, Camille Jenatzy, won the 1903 Gordon Bennett Cup race. The 528-km (328-mile)-long race took place on public roads in Ireland.*

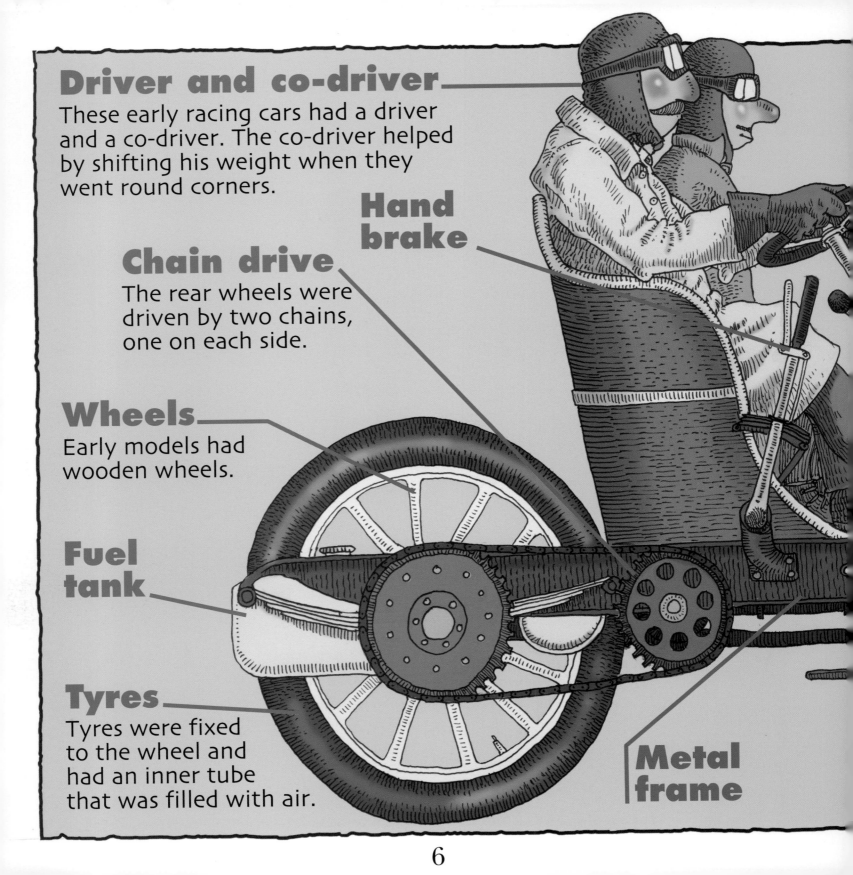

# Driver and co-driver

These early racing cars had a driver and a co-driver. The co-driver helped by shifting his weight when they went round corners.

## Hand brake

## Chain drive

The rear wheels were driven by two chains, one on each side.

## Wheels

Early models had wooden wheels.

## Fuel tank

## Tyres

Tyres were fixed to the wheel and had an inner tube that was filled with air.

## Metal frame

# 1903 Mercedes

## Foot pedals
Pedals were used to slow the car and to make it go faster.

## Engine
This engine provided the power of 60 horses.

## Radiator
Early engines were cooled by water that was pumped through a radiator.

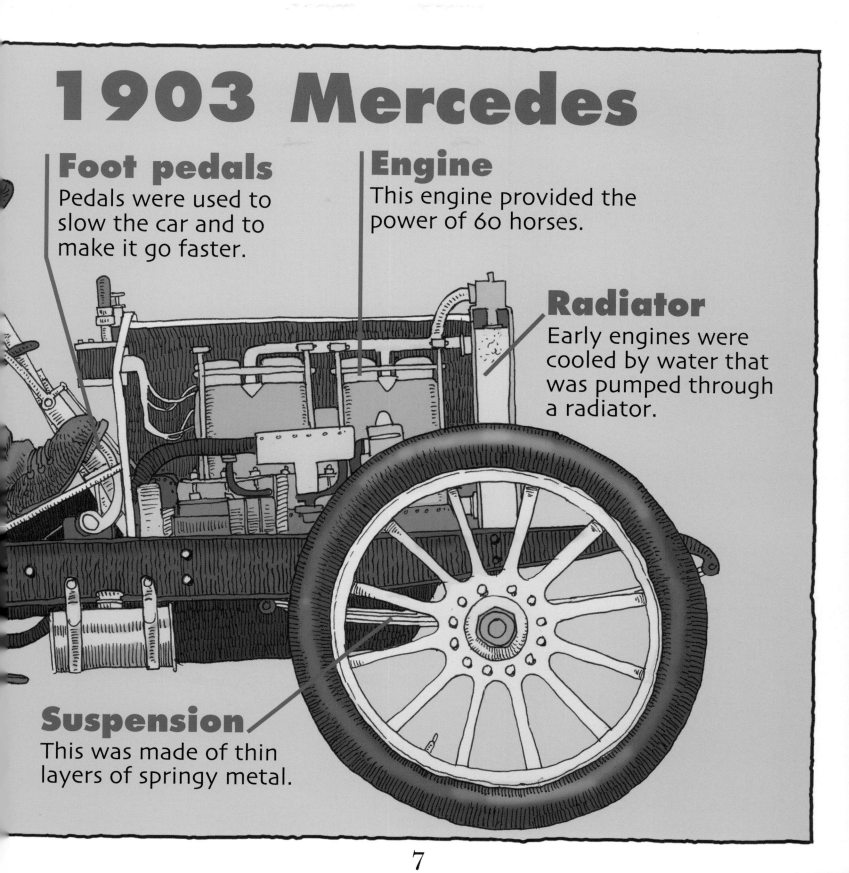

## Suspension
This was made of thin layers of springy metal.

# Single-seaters

The first single-seater racing cars appeared in the 1930s. They were one of the first cars that were specially built to race. The Alfa Romeo P3, shown here, raced in the European Grand Prix races in 1932. The car was very light, weighing just over 680 kilogrammes.

*The Alfa Romeo P3 had an eight cylinder engine that was **supercharged**. Its top speed was 225 kph (140 mph).*

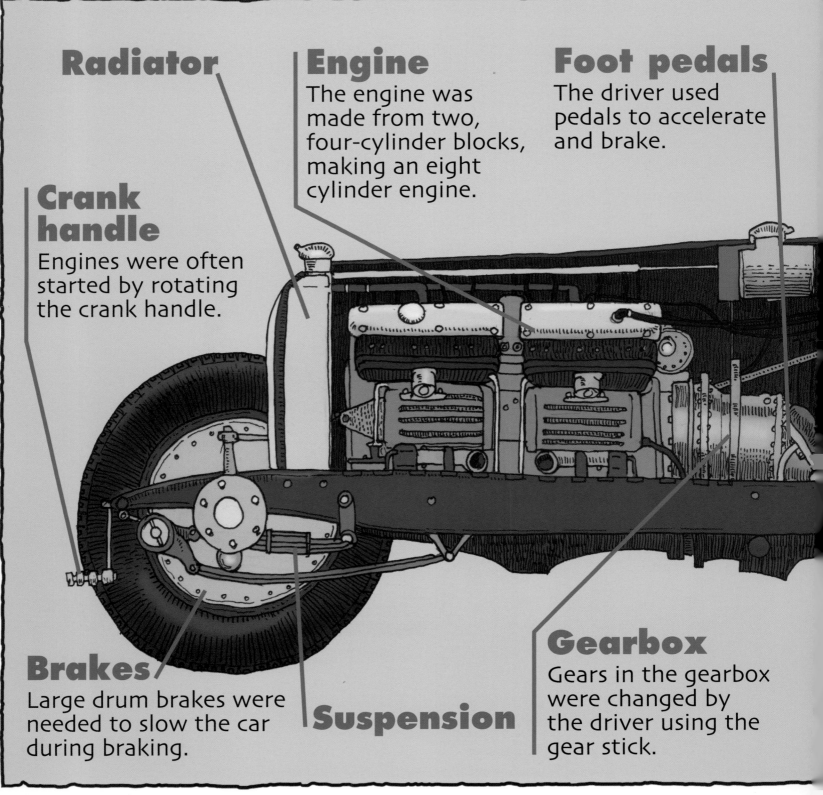

## Radiator

## Engine
The engine was made from two, four-cylinder blocks, making an eight cylinder engine.

## Foot pedals
The driver used pedals to accelerate and brake.

## Crank handle
Engines were often started by rotating the crank handle.

## Brakes
Large drum brakes were needed to slow the car during braking.

## Suspension

## Gearbox
Gears in the gearbox were changed by the driver using the gear stick.

# Alfa Romeo P3

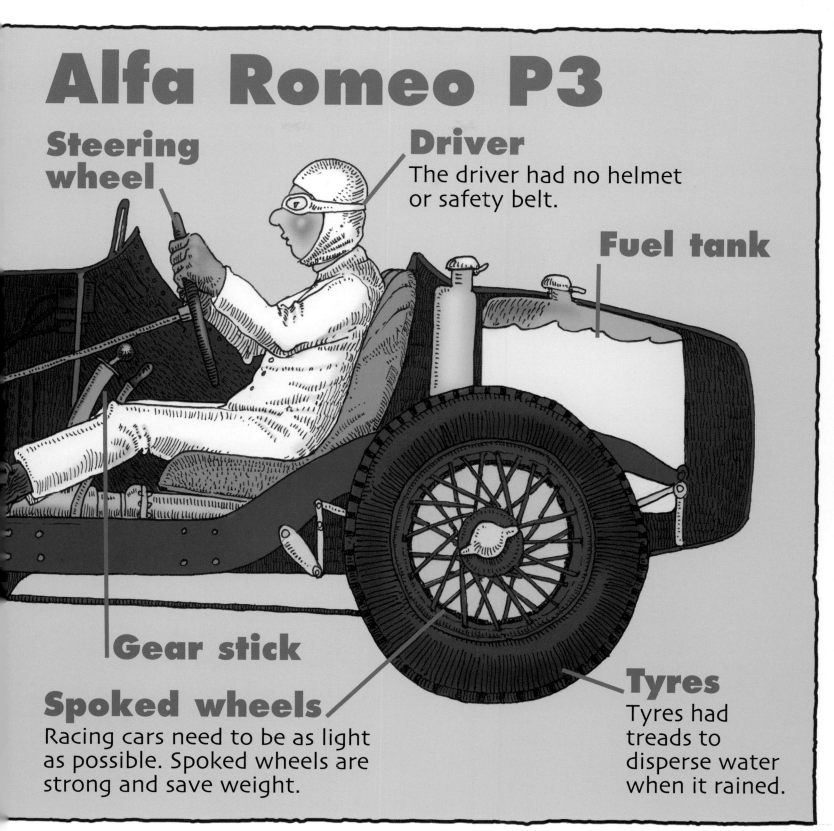

**Steering wheel**

**Driver**
The driver had no helmet or safety belt.

**Fuel tank**

**Gear stick**

**Spoked wheels**
Racing cars need to be as light as possible. Spoked wheels are strong and save weight.

**Tyres**
Tyres had treads to disperse water when it rained.

Modern open-wheelers like this Formula One racing car can be seen racing on specially designed race circuits and on some street circuits in Formula One, IndyCar and NASCAR races.

# Modern Open-wheelers

Open-wheel cars are racing cars with the wheels outside the car's main body and they usually have only one seat. They are built using the latest technology. Engine management, speed and gear shifts are all controlled by the driver using the steering wheel.

# Formula Car

## Front crash structure

The front of the car is designed to crumple to reduce the impact of a crash.

## Pedals

The driver controls the speed and braking with foot pedals.

## Steering wheel

The driver uses the steering wheel to steer and change gear using paddles. There are also buttons and displays to control the engine and rear spoiler.

## Front spoiler

These 'upside down wings' help keep the car's tyres pressed firmly to the track.

## Fire extinguisher

## Electronics

This includes the team radio and transmitter that sends information about the car to engineers in the pit.

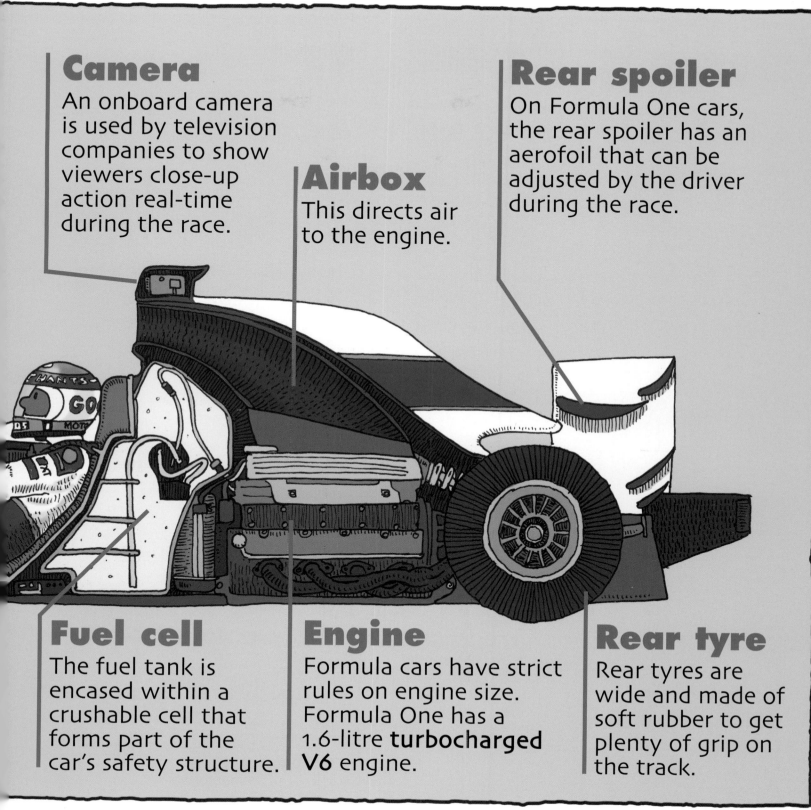

## Camera

An onboard camera is used by television companies to show viewers close-up action real-time during the race.

## Airbox

This directs air to the engine.

## Rear spoiler

On Formula One cars, the rear spoiler has an aerofoil that can be adjusted by the driver during the race.

## Fuel cell

The fuel tank is encased within a crushable cell that forms part of the car's safety structure.

## Engine

Formula cars have strict rules on engine size. Formula One has a 1.6-litre **turbocharged V6** engine.

## Rear tyre

Rear tyres are wide and made of soft rubber to get plenty of grip on the track.

# Stock Car Racers

A stock car racer looks like a standard saloon car. But underneath its lightweight, multi-coloured bodywork is a purpose-built racing machine built to a strict set of rules. Although there are several classes of stock car racing, the cars all look like production cars and they all have similar engines and frames.

In the USA, cars like this Chevrolet race in the NASCAR Sprint Cup Series. They race mostly on oval circuits at a constant speed of around 306 kph (190 mph).

# NASCAR Stock Car

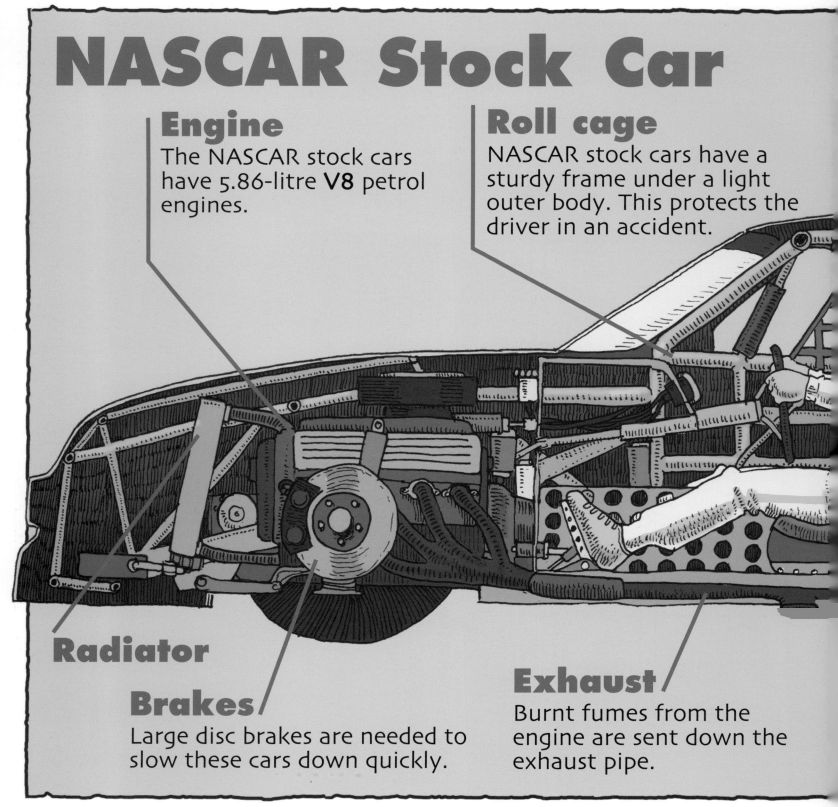

## Engine
The NASCAR stock cars have 5.86-litre **V8** petrol engines.

## Roll cage
NASCAR stock cars have a sturdy frame under a light outer body. This protects the driver in an accident.

## Radiator

## Brakes
Large disc brakes are needed to slow these cars down quickly.

## Exhaust
Burnt fumes from the engine are sent down the exhaust pipe.

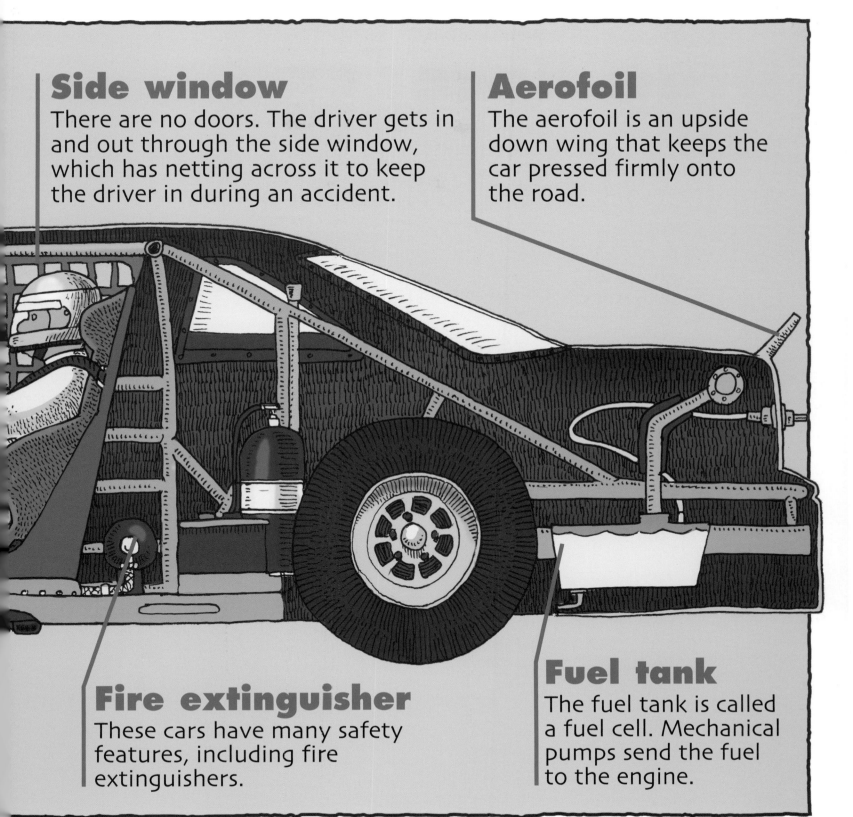

## Side window

There are no doors. The driver gets in and out through the side window, which has netting across it to keep the driver in during an accident.

## Aerofoil

The aerofoil is an upside down wing that keeps the car pressed firmly onto the road.

## Fire extinguisher

These cars have many safety features, including fire extinguishers.

## Fuel tank

The fuel tank is called a fuel cell. Mechanical pumps send the fuel to the engine.

# Drag Racers

Drag racers compete two at a time along a short straight track around 305 metres long. A race typically lasts around 4.5 seconds with cars reaching speeds greater than 530 kph (330 mph). Different specially-built machines compete in these events like this funny car. Flames from burning fuel shoot out of the exhausts as they speed down the track.

Before the race starts each car performs a 'burn out', which heats the large rear tyres and lays rubber down at the beginning of the track. This improves grip when the race starts.

# Funny Car

### Fuel tank
These cars use a special fuel. During a single run, cars can burn as much as 57 litres of fuel.

### Body
The lightweight body is a one piece structure that is lifted up from the font to allow the driver to get in.

### Engine
The V8 engine accelerates the car faster than a jet fighter.

**Disc brake**

**Exhaust pipes**

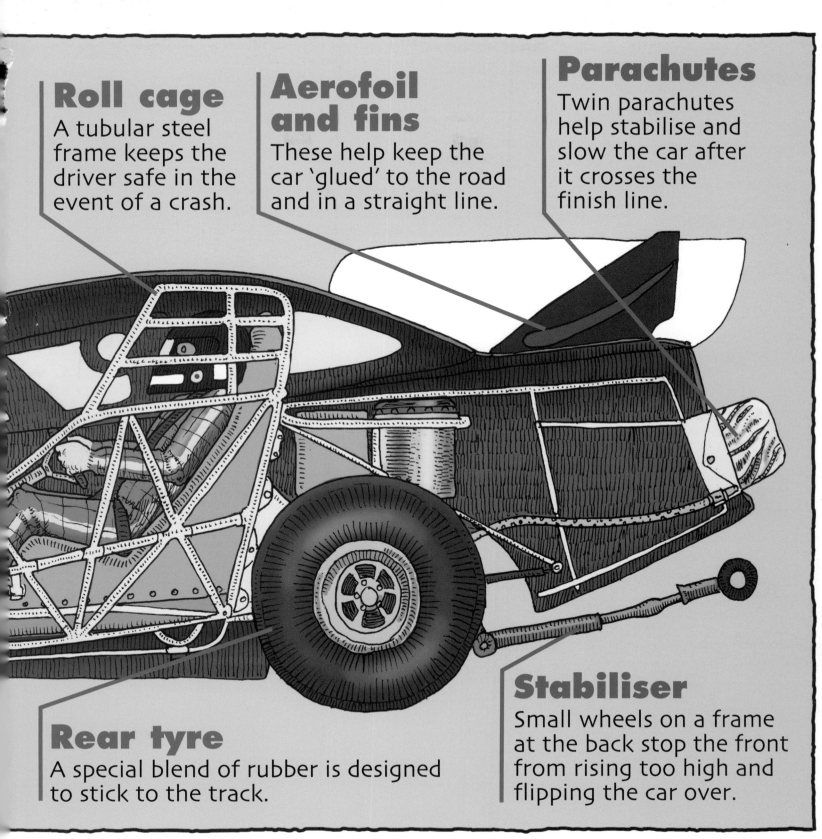

## Roll cage

A tubular steel frame keeps the driver safe in the event of a crash.

## Aerofoil and fins

These help keep the car 'glued' to the road and in a straight line.

## Parachutes

Twin parachutes help stabilise and slow the car after it crosses the finish line.

## Rear tyre

A special blend of rubber is designed to stick to the track.

## Stabiliser

Small wheels on a frame at the back stop the front from rising too high and flipping the car over.

# Glossary

**internal combustion engine**
An engine where the combustion of a fuel and air mixture occurs in a combustion chamber inside the engine.

**supercharged**
Increased power by a supercharger that increases the combustion by squeezing more air into the engine.

**turbocharged**
Increased power by using exhaust fumes to power a turbocharger, which squeezes more air into the engine.

**V6**
An engine layout that has three cylinders on each side forming a v-shape.

**V8**
Similar to a V6 but with four cylinders on each side.

# Index

aerofoil 15, 19, 23
Alfa Romeo 8–11

brake 6, 10, 18, 22

Camille Jenatzy 4
Chevrolet 16–17

drag racers 20

engine 4, 7, 8, 10, 13, 14, 15, 16, 18, 19, 22, 24

exhaust 18, 20, 22, 24

Formula One 12, 15
frame 6, 16, 18, 23
fuel tank 6, 11, 15, 19, 22
funny car 20–23

gears 10, 13, 14
Gordon Bennett Cup 4
Grand Prix 8

IndyCar 12

internal combustion engine 4, 24

Mercedes 4–7

NASCAR 12, 17, 18–19

Open-wheelers 12–15

parachute 23

radiator 7, 10, 18

safety 11, 15, 19
single-seater 8–11
stock car 16–19
suspension 7, 10

tyre 4, 6, 11, 14, 15, 21, 23

wheel 4, 6, 11, 13, 23